$old 4 a $ong

How Music Creators Lost Their Worth, and How to Take It Back

Terrance Lee Sawchuk

Headtraffic Music LLC

Published by Headtraffic Music LLC

Nashville, Tennessee

United States

This book reflects the author's personal experiences and perspectives. It is not intended as legal, financial, or professional advice.

First edition

Printed in the United States of America

www.terrancesawchuk.com

www.sold4asong.com

Contents

Preface

At twenty-seven years old, I found myself staring down my first major publishing deal. On paper, it looked like a dream, a real contract from a major publisher offering a $10,000 advance. But what jumped off the page wasn't the money. It was the math.

That advance wouldn't even cover rent in Toronto. To stay afloat, I'd need a full-time job, maybe two or three. And if I didn't recoup within a year, there would be no second term. Even worse, I'd be repaying that advance using the smallest portion of my future earnings. The songs I had already written, everything on my Schedule A, and anything I'd write during the term would be owned by someone else forever.

Something in me said no.

I went on to turn down every publishing offer for the rest of my career, accepting only administration deals.

Sometimes I walked away months into negotiations, after thousands of dollars in legal fees. I still said no.

Just a few months earlier, I had signed my first major-label artist deal with A&M/PolyGram and had already waded through fifty pages of Catch-22s. I had also just come off a two-year writing and friendship experience with Alanis Morissette, before, during, and after the making of *Jagged Little Pill*, where I saw firsthand how the sausage was made in this industry.

That decision, to remain the owner of my songs, became one of the most important choices of my career. Saying no to my first publishing deal wasn't about confidence. It was about discomfort. I couldn't articulate it at the time, but something about the offer felt like a quiet surrender.

It was the same deal everyone else signed, and that was exactly the problem. I hadn't come this far to give up the very thing I had been depriving myself of for years, worth. So I turned it down. I didn't know where that decision would lead, only that it would define everything that came next.

Where the Story Begins

I grew up in a small Northern Ontario paper-mill town of 5,500 people called Espanola. My later-discovered superpower, then undiagnosed ADHD and dyslexia, made school a daily nightmare. I carried a deep sense of unworthiness and anxiety everywhere I went. I failed ninth-grade music. I skipped more than sixty days of school per year. Eventually, I dropped out.

It took an extremely convincing collision involving my father, my grandmother's piano, a Friday night with my best friend Sean and his piano, an internal voice I can only describe as God, and a song, to snap me awake. I returned to finish high school under a formal contract with the principal. I enrolled in a condensed four-year music program on two instruments and completed it in two years.

Between the ages of sixteen and eighteen, when I wasn't at school or working, I left my basement exactly fourteen times. Every other night, I wrote songs from after dinner until 11 p.m. At eighteen, I said out loud, "I'm going to be a producer." I had no idea what that even meant.

At twenty, I moved to Toronto and enrolled in a recording program that eventually disappointed me, so I left. A few weeks later, I helped start an entirely new school with one of the instructors, John Harris. At first, the school didn't even have a building. When it finally did, we students helped put up the drywall ourselves.

That school became the Harris Institute for the Arts.

Early Lessons

I spent eighteen years in Toronto as a songwriter, producer, engineer, and mixer, working with countless artists and studios, from Moscow to Nashville to Capitol Studios in Los Angeles. I experienced everything from multiple gold and platinum awards to the humbling moment of having a song dropped from *Jagged Little Pill* just months before its release, choosing not to take a co-writing credit on another song from that album, and being forever shaped by Toronto's deeply multicultural creative community.

Those experiences taught me something I would never forget. The level of abundance you reach is directly tied to your sense of self-worth and your willingness to pursue it.

The Journey

In 2007, I felt the pull to move to Nashville. I cashed in my RRSPs, Canada's version of a 401(k), and spent roughly $20,000 over four years on two work visas and a green card. That decision eventually put me back in the position of being tempted with more "starter" publishing deals, and once again, my gut told me to keep going.

Even on the edge of financial ruin, I couldn't find an offer that felt reciprocal. I watched peers sign deals, some prospered, some didn't. I passed on opportunities along the way, but there was always another voice guiding me for reasons I didn't yet understand.

Then, in 2011, luck met preparation.

I co-wrote the two-week Billboard #1, multi-platinum, ASCAP Song of the Year, and Most-Played Country Song of the Decade, "Barefoot Blue Jean Night," with Dylan Altman and Eric Paslay, recorded by Jake Owen (RCA/Sony).

And yet, even with a hit racing up the charts, I was still being offered anorexic, one-sided, ownership-free publishing deals. It was the norm. None of it made sense.

So I relied on my hard-earned understanding of publishing administration and became my own publisher.

That decision, somewhat ironically, landed my personal publishing company on *Billboard*'s Top 100 Publishers of the Year list because of a single song.

At the time, we were still selling CDs and earning sustainable royalty rates. I also knew country music didn't meaningfully sell outside the U.S., Canada, Australia, and parts of the U.K. So I set up administration partnerships directly at the source, not through sub-publishers, in those territories. Whatever pennies I missed internationally were not worth handing over ten percent of my gross earnings.

After the first eighteen months, when the bulk of a hit song's revenue typically arrives, I signed an administration deal with Kobalt Music, a company known for transparency and tech-forward accounting, to track future global royalties.

That single decision saved me over $80,000 in administration fees. Combined with owning my share of the copyright, the song ended up paying as if I'd had two and a half number-one hits.

How important was retaining ownership?

Fifteen years later, that same song still pays like a Top 30 hit every year, and its income has increased 97 percent post-COVID.

Introduction

The use of dollar signs and the number "4" in the title of this book is intentional. It's my quiet homage to the creator who taught me more about artistic sovereignty than anyone else on earth, Prince Rogers Nelson. A man who refused to let the industry define his worth and paid the price upfront so he could rewrite the rules later.

When I first considered writing this book, I went back and forth for months, questioning whether anyone would care, wondering if my voice mattered, and trying to outrun the familiar sense of imposter syndrome that had been stitched into me since childhood. I remember chatting with my friend Mark, who is also an executive business coach, about it. I was in the middle of doubting myself and second-guessing whether I should speak at all. He listened quietly and then said, "If you had the cure to cancer, would you keep it to yourself?"

That hit me harder than he realized. Because in my gut, I knew I was holding something powerful, not a theory, but a lifetime of lived experience. Thirty-five-plus years in the trenches as a songwriter, producer, engineer, mixer, collaborator, and someone who genuinely gives a shit about whether creators ever reap the fruit of their labor, discover their purpose, and use it to serve others.

I've watched too many artists, including myself, get crushed under the weight of a business known for eating its young. But in truth, the deeper wound was always the quiet belief that we weren't worth more. Not because we lacked talent or heart, but because we were never challenged to see our value clearly.

So I stopped questioning. Even when doubt crept in, even when the fear of being judged or misunderstood got loud, something in me refused to stay silent. The desire to serve finally outweighed the fear of being seen. This book is my burden of knowledge laid bare, not as doctrine, not as branding, but as a torch. A way of illuminating the path I wish someone had shown me.

The Moment Everything Shifted

Years ago, I received an email from the booking agent of my friend, artist, and lifelong collaborator, Matt Dusk. A woman had reached out to say that Matt's newest album "Two Shots", an album I had been deeply involved in from a compositional standpoint, especially a song called *Five*, which was the most raw I had ever been as a songwriter, had changed her husband's life.

He was a retired police officer who hadn't spoken a full sentence to his family in decades after witnessing the death of his partner. His now-adult children had grown up, started families of their own, and still had never heard their father speak since they were children. Until that album. He was a big fan of the late Frank Sinatra, and those songs reached him in a place nothing else had touched. His children heard him speak again for the first time since their own childhood, including his grandchildren.

That email stopped me in my tracks. It reminded me, in a way nothing else ever had, that what we create is never just for us. That what I thought was simply me getting my own stories and emotions out was something far greater. I learned right then that songwriting wasn't about me. I was just the first listener.

My music was speaking to me first, awakening something, clarifying something, and only once it moved outward to awaken revelation in others was the cycle complete. That moment changed everything I believed about the purpose of creativity. And once I saw it, I couldn't unsee it.

The Real Work Ahead

I love the look on artists' faces when I tell them there are over 11 million artists on Spotify alone and over 120,000 songs uploaded every single day, not including countless AI-generated songs. But what I love even more is the look on their faces when I follow it with, "And you have zero competition."

Because competition only exists when two things can be compared. And no one else has your story. No one else has your voice. No one else has your scars, your wiring, your experiences, your emotional signature. Your worth isn't measured against anyone else, it's revealed when you reconnect with yourself.

The purpose of this book isn't to overwhelm you with strategy or process. It's not here to teach you how to game an algorithm or mimic what's trending. This book is here to help you remember the core of who you are, the value you've carried all along, the truth that your art has been trying to show you, and the deeper identity your creativity has always been pointing you back toward.

A remembering of sovereignty. A remembering of worth. A remembering that the greatest service you can offer the world begins with awakening yourself.

Because when you reconnect with your blueprint, the real you, something shifts. Your voice strengthens. Your clarity sharpens. Your momentum returns. Your art deepens. Your sense of direction stabilizes. You stop shrinking. You stop disappearing. You stop handing away leverage you never needed to surrender in the first place. You become whole again.

Welcome to the Shift

This book is an invitation. To reclaim your worth. To stop living overextended and overleveraged. To step into your creative life with dignity and clarity. To understand why you've been undervalued and how to take your power back. Most importantly, to awaken something in yourself so you can awaken something in others.

Welcome to the shift. Now let's begin.

Chapter 1

$old 4 a $ong

Definition: Very cheaply, for little money, especially for less than something is worth.

"I know a man... sold a goodly manor for a song."

William Shakespeare, *All's Well That Ends Well*, 3:2

This idiom refers to the pennies given to street singers or the small cost of sheet music, late 1500s. I first heard this saying back in the 1980s. It rolled off the tongue, and you didn't think much about it. But the Shakespeare quote wasn't the origin.

Digging deeper, I found this:

"The phrase originates with a long poem, rather than a song, called *The Faerie Queene*, presented to Queen Elizabeth I by Edmund Spenser. It was regarded as Spenser's most popular work, but Lord Burleigh, the Lord High Treasurer, was unimpressed. When he heard the Queen intended to pay Spenser £100, approximately

$47,000 USD today, for the work, he famously exclaimed, "What! All this for a song?'"

The Queen, much to Burleigh's dismay, insisted on paying the money. The incident was widely reported, and the phrase became English slang, although it came to mean low value rather than high, because of the pennies people tossed to buskers in old London town.

Red Herrings & White Elephants: The Origins of the Phrases We Use Every Day

Albert Jack

A Brief Summary of *The Faerie Queene*

The Faerie Queene is an epic poem following several knights, each representing a specific virtue, on quests to uphold their values. Set in mythical Faerie Land, it is divided into six books, each focused on virtues like Holiness, Temperance, Chastity, Friendship, Justice, and Courtesy. The knights face adversaries and moral challenges throughout their journeys.

The poem also serves as a celebration of Queen Elizabeth I, portrayed as the Faerie Queen herself, and is rich with allegory, Renaissance ideals, and the triumph of virtue.

The Irony

Here's what struck me. The poem is literally about knights on quests to uphold their value, and yet for over 430 years, songwriters and performers have been figuratively or literally undervalued. Some of the greatest creators in history died paupers. Those who recognized the true value of the work, or positioned themselves to benefit from it, reaped the rewards.

So has the perception changed after hundreds of years?

Would This Happen in Any Other Industry?

Imagine this headline. Warren Buffett and Mark Cuban form a songwriting duo. They're thrilled to split $0.0017 per stream, that's if they ever see the money. No one would take it seriously.

Yet creators, songwriters, producers, and artists accept this reality every day.

We've all heard it.

"It's good promotion for you."

"We don't have a budget, but you'll get exposure."

"We're considering giving you a career."

"If you bring a lawyer, the deal is off."

Many of us have lived through publishers posturing to make you feel unworthy to get a better cut of the deal, executives taking ownership or publishing without consent, and many claiming songwriting credit by pressure or force. This culture is centuries old.

• • •

Creators Must Reverse-Engineer This Thinking

If you remember one thing from this chapter, remember this:

"The wealthiest entities in the music business and big tech acquire copyright, publishing, masters, data, emails, and algorithms, and artists do everything in their power to sell or give them all away."

Creators spend their careers giving all of it away. This is not because creators lack the ability to manage their business. It's because they've been conditioned to undervalue themselves, historically, psychologically, and structurally.

Stephen Foster, An Early Lesson in Value

Stephen Foster, 1826 to 1864, composer of "Camptown Races" and "Oh! Susanna," was one of the first songwriters to demand additional royalties for sheet music. Before that, songwriters received one-time buyouts, and the publisher kept everything forever.

Foster negotiated payments between $25 and $200 per song, while all future earnings went to the publisher. Foster had 38 cents to his name when he died.

Value Creation

Foster demonstrated:

Worth, he believed his music deserved more.

Leverage, he recognized that he was the inventor and the CEO.

Streamlining, he created an ecosystem that paid him while he slept.

Sustaining, he changed the structure of songwriter compensation.

His decisions planted seeds for modern royalty systems, even though the business still finds ways to overleverage and underpay creators.

Chapter Summary

- The phrase "sold for a song" has historically meant undervalued, a theme running through over 430 years of creative history.

- Songwriters and performers have long been treated as low-value assets, despite producing enormous cultural, health, and economic value.

- Modern musicians face the same issues as those in the 1500s, low pay, exploitative contracts, and systemic undervaluing.

- Creators routinely give away what corporations spend billions to acquire, copyright, ownership, identity, data, and leverage.

- Stephen Foster's early push for royalties highlights how rare it has been for creators to be compensated fairly.

- Society conditions creators to measure their worth externally rather than internally, contributing to chronic undervaluing.

- Reversing this cycle requires awareness, ownership, and value creation, choosing not to be sold for a song.

Chapter 2

And You Think You're Just Writing a Song

"Amazing Grace," possibly the most revered song in Black culture, carries a profound irony. The lyric was written by John Newton, a white former captain of a slave ship who converted to Christianity and later came to regret his role in the slave trade. The melody is believed to have come from a hymn titled *New Britain*, with the composer unknown. Together, they formed an anthem of grace, redemption, forgiveness, and the transformative power of faith.

"Born in the U.S.A.," written and performed by Bruce Springsteen, is often mistaken for a flag-waving anthem when, in reality, it is a searing commentary on veterans, their mistreatment, and the disillusionment of the American Dream.

"Strange Fruit," made famous by Billie Holiday, is one of those songs that doesn't entertain, it interrupts. It stops time, strips away illusion, and holds a mirror to the world.

• • •

Strange Fruit, When a Song Becomes a Reckoning

In the mid-1930s, Abel Meeropol, a Jewish schoolteacher and poet from the Bronx, wrote a poem titled *Bitter Fruit* after seeing a newspaper photograph of a lynching in Marion, Indiana. The image haunted him, two Black men hanging from a tree, surrounded by a cheering crowd.

Meeropol set the poem to music and performed it with his wife at small union and left-wing gatherings in New York. One of those performances caught the attention of Barney Josephson, the owner of Café Society, the first integrated nightclub in America. Josephson believed music could challenge injustice as powerfully as it could entertain, and he immediately thought of his headlining singer, Billie Holiday.

Holiday was already a star at Café Society, known for her truth as an artist. Josephson introduced her to Meeropol. They sat together as Abel and his wife performed "Strange Fruit" live for her. When they finished, Billie sat silent for a long moment, then said softly, "It reminds me of my father."

Her father, musician Clarence Holiday, had died after being denied medical treatment at a segregated hospital, a wound she never forgot. That connection made the song personal. She felt it in her bones. She agreed to perform it, knowing full well the danger. Singing about lynching in 1939 was not just controversial, it was life-threatening.

At Café Society, the lights would dim to black. A single spotlight illuminated her face. No drinks were served. No one dared to speak. And then, “Southern trees bear a strange fruit, blood on the leaves and blood at the root...” The room froze. You could feel centuries of pain, dignity, and unspoken truth vibrating through her voice.

When she finished, she left the stage in silence, no encore, no applause. Just the echo of a nation forced to face itself. “Strange Fruit” wasn’t simply a song, it was a reckoning. It exposed what society tried to hide. It transformed art into activism long before the word activism existed. For a few minutes each night, in a smoky basement club, Billie Holiday turned entertainment into empathy. She made audiences feel what headlines refused to say.

When Power Felt Threatened

When “Strange Fruit” hit the airwaves, the reaction was explosive. Critics called it “the beginning of the civil rights movement in song.” But not everyone applauded. The U.S. government, specifically the Federal Bureau of Narcotics, saw something else, a Black woman with too much influence.

Harry Anslinger, the bureau’s head, was a notorious racist and one of the most powerful men in America. He despised jazz, drugs, and especially outspoken Black artists who challenged the status quo. When “Strange Fruit” gained attention, Anslinger considered Billie Holiday a threat. He openly called her “the symbol of everything wrong with America.”

He assigned federal agents to follow, harass, and build a case against her. His memos described her as "defiant," "insolent," and "a menace." Make no mistake, this wasn't about drugs. It was about control. Billie Holiday had used her voice to expose a truth the government wanted buried.

In 1947, Anslinger sent one of his Black agents, Jimmy Fletcher, to infiltrate Holiday's circle and entrap her. Fletcher grew close to her, even admired her, but ultimately betrayed her under orders.

She was arrested for heroin possession, convicted, and sent to prison for a year and a day. Upon release, the government revoked her cabaret card, making it illegal for her to perform in any New York club that served alcohol, effectively cutting off her income.

Imagine that, one of the greatest vocalists in American history, banned from performing.

Later, as she lay dying in a hospital, weak, impoverished, with only $0.70 left in her bank account, federal agents handcuffed her to her bed, guarded her room, and prevented visitors from bringing medication. They even took away her record player. She died in 1959, under police watch. Her final word was, "No."

That song terrified the government because it made people feel. It forced white America to confront the brutality it normalized.

And in Billie Holiday's raw, wounded, unwavering voice, the truth could not be ignored. By trying to silence her, they immortalized her. Every time a truth-teller sings today, every time an artist risks reputation or safety to expose injustice, they walk the path Billie Holiday carved.

She didn't have a platform. She was the platform. "Strange Fruit" proved that a single song could shake the foundations of power, not through volume, but through truth.

Work Songs, Music as Survival and Resistance

Work songs sung by enslaved Africans were more than music to pass the time, they were lifelines. They carried culture, communication, spiritual resilience, and often coded instructions for survival or escape.

Rhythmic and Communal Function

Work songs kept enslaved laborers physically synchronized and emotionally connected. The call-and-response format allowed a leader to call and the group to respond, creating unity while performing exhausting, repetitive tasks.

Emotional Expression

These songs expressed grief, hope, love, longing, resistance, and even joy. They provided a psychological release that enslaved people were otherwise denied.

Spiritual Influence

Many work songs drew from Christian hymns fused with African spiritual traditions, becoming early forms of spirituals centered around deliverance, salvation, and hope.

Hidden Meanings and Codes

Many work songs contained coded messages that enslaved people understood, but overseers did not.

The Underground Railroad

“Follow the Drinking Gourd”

The “drinking gourd” referred to the Big Dipper, pointing to the North Star. The lyrics were literal escape instructions.

“Wade in the Water”

This spiritual advised escapees to walk through rivers to throw off bloodhounds tracking their scent.

Songs as covert messaging, melodies that communicated meaning, often hidden in plain sight:

- meeting times
- warnings
- escape routes
- moments of opportunity

Defiance, Longing, and Hope

Even without overt rebellion, these songs offered spiritual defiance.

“No More Auction Block for Me”

A direct cry against the slave trade, expressing a yearning for freedom.

"Steal Away to Jesus"

Sung to signal secret religious meetings or to share whispered plans of resistance.

Cultural Legacy

Work songs are the roots of:

- Blues
- Gospel
- Jazz
- Soul
- Rock
- R&B

They remain a living testament to resilience, faith, ingenuity, and resistance. These songs were not just survival tools, they were blueprints for liberation.

Songs That Changed Society

Other society-shaping songs of immeasurable value and impact include:

- "We Shall Overcome," Pete Seeger
- "Blowin' in the Wind," Bob Dylan

- "Respect," Aretha Franklin
- "Imagine," John Lennon
- "Redemption Song," Bob Marley
- "Fight the Power," Public Enemy
- "What's Goin' On," Marvin Gaye

The Economic Reality Behind the Music

My friend Patrick Raines, retired Dean of Business at Belmont University in Nashville, was responsible for assembling the team that created the first-ever economic impact study on music in Nashville, Tennessee.

That study revealed something extraordinary. Music was generating **$9.7 billion annually** for the city by 2013. But the most important insight was not the headline number. It was **who actually benefited from that value**.

Avenue Bank recognized the significance of the findings immediately. They understood that music was not just culture or entertainment, it was a powerful economic engine rooted in intellectual property. So they aligned their services with the music ecosystem, offering financial products designed for music businesses, rights holders, and infrastructure owners.

In 2015, Avenue Financial Holdings filed for an IPO, raising $30 million and positioning itself as a key financial player in the music sector. Their strategy was clear, leverage the true value of music to raise capital, expand services, and anchor the company in an industry whose impact far exceeded its public perception.

But here is the insight most people miss.

The greatest beneficiaries of Nashville's music economy were not the creators. They were the entities in positions of **ownership**.

Those who owned catalogs, publishing, masters, real estate, venues, and financial instruments captured the long-term upside. Those closest to creation, songwriters, musicians, producers, engineers, often participated only in short-term income, not enduring wealth.

You can see this pattern even inside the walls of Nashville's most respected, full-service recording studios.

In the 1980s, professional recording studios in Nashville charged premium hourly rates for world-class rooms and staff engineers. Decades later, those same studios are charging roughly the same hourly rates. Meanwhile, the value extracted from the music recorded inside those rooms has exploded. **The result is that the music community can no longer afford the cost of prime real estate in downtown Nashville. The very people who built the city's tourism and population boom can no longer maintain it. That's why I now call Music Row, Condo Row.**

In other words, **the price of making the music has stayed mostly flat**, while the value extracted from owning the music has grown exponentially.

According to the Nashville Area Chamber of Commerce:

- The $9.7 billion figure reflects data from 2013
- It does not include the population boom, tourism surge, or infrastructure growth Nashville has experienced since
- The total economic impact of music was $9.7 billion annually
- Over 56,000 jobs were supported by music
- More than $3.2 billion in labor income was generated each year

And every single penny of that impact exists because of a song.

No song, no musicians.

No song, no producers.

No song, no engineers.

No song, no publishers.

No song, no labels.

No song, no studios.

No song, no managers.

No song, no agents.

No song, no promoters.

No song, no tours.

No song, no Broadway.

No song, no festivals.

No song, no music tourism.

No music tourism, no billion-dollar creative economy.

No billion-dollar creative economy, no real estate boom, no IPOs built on the backs of creators.

That's the actual worth.

At the time of this writing, Spotify's stock trades above $700 per share. For the average songwriter, you may have been financially better off buying $1,000 of Spotify stock at $18 a share than attempting to collect payment from Spotify for your streams.

The world knows the value of music.

Banks know it.

Investors know it.

Tech companies know it.

Wall Street knows it.

The only ones who were never taught their own worth are the inventors.

And that is why this conversation, and this book, exist.

When Music Stops Being Art, and Becomes Medicine

If music can interrupt injustice, awaken conscience, create billions of dollars for music users, and move nations to reckon with themselves, then it shouldn't surprise us that it can also heal the human brain.

And yet, this is where the irony deepens. Because even when music is proven to restore movement, memory, speech, emotional regulation, and dignity, even when neuroscience confirms its power, it is still routinely undervalued.

Not because it doesn't work. But because it's music.

I was recently joined on my podcast by Dr. Concetta Tomaino, Connie, a pioneer in the field of clinical music therapy and neurological rehabilitation. Her life's work sits at the intersection of neuroscience, medicine, and music, and it offers one of the clearest confirmations of music's true worth I've ever encountered.

Music therapy, as a profession, formally emerged in the United States in the 1950s, when doctors and educators noticed something remarkable, patients who could not speak, move, or engage cognitively would suddenly come alive when exposed to music. Children who could not process language responded to rhythm.

Veterans with PTSD became present. Patients with Alzheimer's and Parkinson's accessed memories long thought lost. These weren't emotional anecdotes. They were repeatable, observable outcomes.

Modern neuroscience now understands why. Music doesn't live in one part of the brain. It activates nearly all of it. Timing and rhythm engage motor systems. Pitch engages temporal regions. Melody and harmony stimulate memory networks. Emotion links directly to autobiographical recall.

Music is processed as pattern, and pattern recognition is foundational to survival, language, bonding, and meaning. Even before birth, the human brain is learning rhythm.

That's why a lullaby calms a child. Why a song can trigger a memory faster than words. Why the first note of a familiar melody can collapse decades into a single emotional moment.

In clinical settings, this power is not abstract. Dr. Tomaino described patients written off as unreachable, catatonic, agitated, cognitively "gone," who began singing lyrics they hadn't spoken in years. Veterans learned to reconnect with suppressed emotion through improvisation and rhythm. Parkinson's patients could suddenly walk freely as long as the rhythm was present.

Music doesn't just soothe the brain. It organizes it.

And yet, despite decades of research, peer-reviewed science, and documented outcomes, music therapy still struggles for basic recognition and reimbursement.

Insurance companies hesitate. Institutions undervalue the service. Music therapists are routinely asked to justify their rates in ways other healthcare professionals are not.

Why? Because somewhere deep in our cultural wiring, music is still treated as extra. Optional. Decorative.

The same bias that tells a songwriter they should be grateful for "exposure" tells a music therapist their work shouldn't cost much. Different fields. Same distortion of worth.

Worth Is Proven, But Still Negotiated

This is the contradiction at the heart of the creative economy.

Music can:

- awaken memory in dementia patients
- restore movement in neurological disease
- regulate trauma responses
- support early childhood development
- shape identity, culture, and resistance

And yet, the people who create and apply it are consistently asked to accept less.

As Dr. Tomaino put it plainly, music therapists face the same battle as artists, learning to articulate value in a world that assumes music should be cheap simply because it feels natural.

Plumbers don't apologize for their invoices. Mechanics aren't asked to work for exposure. But creatives and healers using music are expected to discount their worth.

That disconnect isn't accidental. It's historical. From enslaved people embedding escape routes into songs, to Billie Holiday risking her life to sing the truth, to neuroscientists proving music restores function, music has always carried enormous value for society.

But the people closest to it are taught to undervalue themselves.

The Quiet Truth

When you look at the historical reality for music creators, overleveraged, undercompensated, often paying for it with their own health and nervous systems, it becomes easy to mistake impact for income.

Music gives everything. Creators are taught to accept whatever remains.

That irony is what this chapter exists to expose. Because whether music is changing laws, healing trauma, or restoring dignity to someone the world has written off, it is never "just a song."

Chapter Summary

- Music has shaped culture, carried resistance, preserved memory, healed trauma, and restored function where medicine alone could not reach.
- From protest songs to spirituals, from neurological rehabilitation to emotional awakening, music proves its worth again and again, often in the most extreme human conditions.

• And yet, those who create and apply music are still asked to justify their value.

• This chapter reveals a truth the system prefers to ignore. If music is powerful enough to heal the brain and confront injustice, then the problem has never been music's value. The problem has always been who is allowed to claim it.

Chapter 3

I Just Wanna Be Unique, Like Everyone Else

As I mentioned earlier, I love telling artists there are over 11 million artists on Spotify alone. And you have zero competition.

Society doesn't seem designed to nurture uniqueness. In fact, it often does the opposite, encouraging us to operate on the same mental software, chasing the same signals of approval, safety, and validation.

"We're trained by society, social media, and school to measure ourselves against ideals or to compare ourselves to other people. We're always looking outside of ourselves to get validation, rather than learning how to validate ourselves."

— **Benjamin Hardy**, *The Gap and the Gain*

But that's not how we were created. So why do we spend so much time building our lives and careers on foundations that were never meant for us?

A **Tony Robbins** podcast featuring **Dr. Bruce Lipton** became a tipping point for me on this subject. Dr. Lipton explains that **much of our lives, often cited as up to 95 percent**, is driven by subconscious programming acquired before the age of seven, programming that comes from parents, culture, school systems, religion, and trauma.

That realization landed hard. It meant that for most of us, programming, not creativity, became the default operating system. And suddenly, a lot made sense. Why authenticity feels dangerous. Why standing out feels risky. Why so many creators struggle with fear when they try to express something true.

That programming gets downloaded early, almost like malware, and then quietly runs in the background, shaping decisions we believe are conscious choices. Dr. Lipton often says that movement is the secret to life. Action is not optional, it's biological. Signal plus response creates motion. Life itself depends on how we respond to the world around us. Your DNA is not destiny.

Think of it like a library of blueprints. Just because a book exists in the library doesn't mean it has to be read. The environment determines which books get opened.

Lipton's work shows that genes don't activate themselves. They are switched on by proteins responding to signals from the environment, including physical surroundings, emotional states, and belief systems.

Your consciousness influences the biochemical environment that tells your body, and your creative instincts, how to respond. In other words, you are not controlled by your genes. Your responses help determine which parts of you come online.

The framework is simple. Thoughts. Environment. Emotions.

You are not a victim of these forces, but you are shaped by them.

When I look back at my song catalog, which songs were covered, which weren't, which changed my life, and which quietly disappeared, I can see something clearly. I can see exactly where I was stepping outside my God given unique blueprint.

I can also see the moments when I stopped trying to please anyone, when I trusted my instincts, created without attachment, and allowed myself to simply be. Those songs became the ones that lasted.

There were moments when I thought, who cares if it's too long? Too slow? Too different? I could hear the song fully formed in my mind, and my only job was to follow it.

That's when things changed.

People often say that living spiritually, trusting God, or following a purpose is inspiring, but then add, "I still have to pay the bills."

I understand that tension. But consider this. What if tapping into your truth, beyond the programming you've been running most of your life, doesn't subtract from abundance, but reorganizes it? What if alignment doesn't remove responsibility, but clarifies direction? What if everything was happening for you, not to you, and all you have to do is trust it?

I've come to believe that the key is following truth with zero attachment to outcome. History is full of creators who never saw the value of their work recognized in their lifetime, not because the work lacked value, but because the world wasn't ready yet.

The struggle isn't talent. It's not effort. It's the stories we've been running. And the irony is this. Those stories often become the raw material for our art. If we follow our own breadcrumb trail honestly enough, we may discover that we were never meant to compete, only to contribute. Not to conform, but to collaborate. Not to impress, but to awaken.

Chapter Summary

• You have no competition because no one else carries your blueprint.

• Most fear around authenticity comes from subconscious programming, not lack of ability.

• Creativity thrives when environment, emotion, and belief align.

• The most impactful work often comes from honesty, not strategy.

- Following truth without attachment changes how value shows up, creatively and materially.

- Awakening yourself is often the first step toward awakening others.

Chapter 4

Home of The Free?

It is worth examining why unions exist for nearly every role in music, television, and film, except for the actual creators of the song itself. There is also a strong case to be made for music producers and engineers.

Below is a list of entities in the entertainment industry that benefit from union representation:

Musicians and Arrangers: American Federation of Musicians

Singers: SAG-AFTRA

Actors: SAG-AFTRA

Stage Workers: IATSE, the International Alliance of Theatrical Stage Employees

Directors: Directors Guild of America

Producers: Producers Guild of America

Screenplay Writers: Writers Guild of America

Now compare that with a list of professions whose income is set, in whole or in part, by the federal government in Washington:

Court Reporters: Rates are set by the Judicial Conference of the United States, the policy-making body for federal courts.

Minimum Wage Workers: The federal minimum wage is set by Congress and enforced by the Department of Labor.

Songwriters: Royalty rates are set by the Copyright Royalty Board, a panel of three judges appointed by the Librarian of Congress.

The Copyright Royalty Board consists of three judges tasked with determining mechanical royalty rates for songwriters. In practice, these judges operate under intense pressure from lobbyists and third-party users with massive financial interests. Under the current structure, it is illegal for songwriters to form a traditional union.

That's right. In the land of the free and the home of the brave, the actual inventor of the song, the asset every other participant in the music economy relies on, is the only one legally prohibited from collective bargaining.

My stance is simple. The government should play no role in determining our rights or rates. Like every other sector of the entertainment industry, songwriters should be able to manage their own lives and livelihoods in a true free market.

• • •

Why Songwriters Can't Form a Union

The Short Answer

Songwriters are legally blocked from forming a traditional union because U.S. antitrust law treats them as independent businesses, not workers.

Here is the breakdown.

1. Songwriters Are Classified as Independent Contractors

Under U.S. law, unions exist for employees. Songwriters are legally classified as:

Independent contractors

Small businesses

Owners of intellectual property

Even if you are broke, unrecouped, signed to a publisher, or entirely dependent on platforms like Spotify or radio, the law still views you as a rights holder, not a worker. That single classification closes the door to unionization.

2. Antitrust Law Is the Real Blocker

If songwriters attempted to unionize in the traditional sense, the government would claim they are competitors coordinating prices, an antitrust violation under the Sherman Act.

If songwriters collectively said:

“We won’t license below this rate.”

“We demand better streaming terms.”

“We won’t accept these contracts.”

It would be treated the same as oil companies colluding on price.

This is why musicians can coordinate, singers can coordinate, publishers can coordinate, PROs can coordinate, record labels can coordinate, DSPs can coordinate, Live Nation can coordinate, broadcast radio can coordinate, but the inventors cannot.

3. PROs Are a Narrow and Heavily Restricted Exception

Performance Rights Organizations, ASCAP, BMI, and SESAC, exist only because of specific legal carve-outs and consent decrees.

Even then:

Rates are often set by courts, not creators

Their scope is limited to performance royalties

They cannot strike

They cannot refuse licenses collectively

PROs are not unions. They are regulated collection agencies.

. . .

4. Why Actors and Screenwriters Can Unionize, but Songwriters Can't

Actors and screenwriters are treated as labor-for-hire. They are employees on a production and do not own the finished intellectual property.

Songwriters, by contrast:

Own the asset

License it repeatedly

Generate downstream revenue indefinitely

That ownership flips the legal logic from labor law to competition law. Ironically, owning your work removes your right to collective bargaining.

5. Congress Knows This, and Has Done Almost Nothing

This is why we see repeated attempts at limited reform, such as the American Music Fairness Act or narrow antitrust exemptions for creators. These efforts are consistently met with aggressive lobbying from Big Tech, broadcasters, and media conglomerates. If creators gain collective leverage, upstream margins collapse.

. . .

6. The Brutal Truth

Songwriters exist in a legal no-man's land:

Too independent to be protected

Too fragmented to have leverage

Too valuable to ignore

Too powerless to negotiate

This is why unions are blocked, strikes are illegal, collective refusal is criminalized, and "promotion" is routinely used to justify nonpayment.

7. The Only Viable Paths Forward, Non-Union

The future does not lie in unions. It lies in economic architecture:

Collective ownership structures, co-ops, pooled rights, funds

Artist-owned platforms

Direct-to-fan economics

Catalog leverage without forced sales

Legislative carve-outs, slow and political

Parallel financial systems

Not unions. Systems.

. . .

A Warning Shot from Washington

In early 2025, a quiet but monumental moment unfolded in Washington, D.C. The head of the U.S. Copyright Office, Shira Perlmutter, publicly questioned whether artificial intelligence companies should be allowed to train their models on copyrighted music without permission or payment.

Within days of publishing a report that raised that question, she was fired on the direction of Donald Trump.

Perlmutter, appointed in 2020, was the Register of Copyrights, the nation's top copyright official. Under her leadership, the Copyright Office released an extensive study examining whether scraping millions of songs to train generative AI systems could legally qualify as fair use. Her conclusion was simple. It wasn't that clear.

She warned that AI systems trained on copyrighted works without authorization might cross the line from innovation into infringement. In plain language, if your song helped train an AI, that AI might owe you something.

Two days later, she was terminated. No hearing. No press conference. Just gone.

Those inside the music and policy world understood the message. Challenge the big tech agenda. Challenge the president's donors. Protect creators. Lose your job.

Perlmutter later filed a legal challenge, arguing her removal was unlawful and that the Copyright Office should remain independent, not subject to political retaliation.

Her firing didn't just silence one official. It marked a turning point. The war between creative ownership and machine consumption had officially begun.

Now do you see why I am building awareness around individual ownership, protection, leverage, streamlining, and long-term sustainability?

In the United States, songwriters are uniquely regulated. Unlike most professions, which function within open markets or collective bargaining, songwriter income is governed by rates set by a federally appointed board, inherently exposed to political and governmental influence.

In practice, the Copyright Royalty Board, whether it intends to or not, functions less as a guardian of creators and more as a volume knob for the companies that profit from music.

Music and entertainment are deeply interconnected. Musicians, singers, stage workers, directors, producers, and screenwriters all rely on songs in some way to make a living. Yet songwriters alone are denied a true free-market economy in the land of capitalism.

The United States is also one of the only countries that does not pay songwriters or score composers for theatrical film performances under the outdated movie theater exemption. It is similarly one of the few countries that does not pay properly and transparently for performance royalties from concerts.

I had my publisher and PRO investigate why my songs earned only hundreds of dollars while artists played sold-out shows for over a decade. Artists and their representatives are required to submit setlists to promoters. Promoters are required to pay a percentage of live show earnings to PROs so songwriters can be paid for the use of their music. Somewhere in that chain, the money never reached my PRO.

I can assure you that some of the biggest concerts in the world are not paying these live royalties properly, and sometimes not at all.

Chapter Summary

• Examines the unique regulatory framework governing songwriters in the United States

• Contrasts the songwriter system with unionized sectors of the entertainment industry

• Explains how antitrust law and government-set rates limit songwriter leverage

• Shows how technological disruption has intensified these imbalances

• Highlights the paradox of a system that depends entirely on songwriters while offering them little power

• Explores how emerging technologies may enable new economic models

- Points toward alternatives rooted in ownership, autonomy, and sustainability
- Challenges reliance on outdated regulatory structures in favor of future-facing solutions

Chapter 5

We Are A Walking Asset Class

Just before COVID hit, songwriters found themselves in a new era, the boom of Wall Street investors and pension funds buying song catalogs at scale. Once again, I found myself considering the idea of selling my songs. This time, however, I had just spent several years working on affordable housing solutions with an individual whose net worth exceeded a billion dollars. Let's just say I learned more about money in those two years than I had in my entire life.

What I learned was simple. Investors of this caliber never spend a dime unless something is deeply undervalued. That realization led me to ask a critical question. What do they know that I don't?

Investors were entering a sector that had been dramatically undervalued for decades. The first tier consisted of struggling creatives, songwriters who may have once flourished but now could barely pay the rent, often selling equipment just to survive. In that position, many understandably accept whatever is offered.

The second tier included highly successful songwriters who chose to sell primarily to reduce capital gains exposure, free up liquidity, and position themselves to repeat their success with significant cash on hand.

The third tier consisted of the Dylans and Springsteens of the world, who had no intention of leaving money on the table and preferred to spend it while they were still alive.

But the real reason investors were so hungry for music copyrights had little to do with sentiment and everything to do with what was coming next. Changes in copyright law. Shifts in market share. Improvements in royalty collection efficiency driven by technology.

Equally important, investors classify music royalties as uncorrelated assets, assets not tied to the stock market or broader economic cycles, making them ideal for portfolio diversification. This combination of extreme undervaluation and long-term stability triggered a tsunami of catalog acquisitions.

Meanwhile, I was sitting on a catalog that included a legacy country copyright, or, as I like to call it, a Redneck Picasso, weighing the pros and cons of selling once again. History told me there were long-term benefits to holding on, but selling could have dramatically changed my life financially.

Right or wrong, my gut kept saying this. If these investors only buy extremely undervalued, uncorrelated assets, why not let them blaze the trail toward increasing song earnings and benefit from their leverage instead of surrendering ownership?

Here's the key insight. It costs creators almost nothing to create a song. Our time. Our skills. Some equipment. In many cases, we're even paid an advance to create the asset. Meanwhile, investors must spend hundreds of millions, or even billions, to acquire what we create.

We produce one of the most resilient asset classes in existence at minimal cost, while others pay a fortune to access it.

Can you think of a better asset than one that's relatively immune to economic swings and costs almost nothing to produce?

In fact, creators may be better off diversifying their own portfolios by buying equity in the very companies and platforms investing in our music. For years, I've encouraged songwriters to consider borrowing against their royalty income instead of selling their catalogs outright.

Bring in investors or lenders who front capital based on your earnings. Structure the deal so the asset generates enough cash flow to service the debt, and suddenly you're living off non-taxable loan proceeds instead of paying capital gains. All the while, you still own your songs and masters.

I felt a sense of validation when The Weeknd borrowed over a billion dollars against his assets instead of selling them, preserving ownership of his copyrights. This is the era I've been waiting for, one where creators begin thinking like investors. The ability to create uncorrelated assets and leverage them intelligently is incredibly powerful.

Which raises a bigger question. What's stopping creators from building their own investment vehicles? Instead of selling our catalogs, why not pool a portion of our net royalties into a collective financial structure, essentially the same model Wall Street uses with our work? This approach could create security and leverage while increasing the overall value of our catalogs, without giving up ownership.

And why stop there? A portion of those earnings could fund lobbying, legal support, financial assistance, and even a group healthcare plan. Oops. Did I just outline the foundation of a union without legally being a union? More on that later. This wouldn't take much to bring to fruition.

It's largely a matter of education and coordination. There it is. The blueprint. Together, we can become both creators and investors, leveraging our music instead of being leveraged by it.

Since then, many of my peers have sold their catalogs and made significant money. In nearly every case, it was the publisher who sold the copyright without the creator's consent, because the publisher owned the rights.

As I write this, royalty payment reforms and streaming growth projections suggest global subscribers could rise from 500 million to more than 2 billion in the next five to seven years.

My own royalty earnings have increased significantly since the investor gold rush began. That number could continue to rise, or it could fall. Either way, I won't be selling. These songs will be passed on to my family and the next generation.

I'm not claiming my path is the only or best one. Only that I felt called to take it. And if other songwriters and artists want to explore this route, I can help them do so.

I share this story because it represents my journey, how I learned enough to earn the right to speak about ownership, leverage, streamlining, and sustaining a career.

After attending SXSW 2024, I was struck by how aggressively artists were being leveraged by tech solutions, even after more than 30 years in the business. I kept thinking, shouldn't it be the other way around?

I returned to Music City with an itch I couldn't ignore. How do I share what I've learned and help artists build sustainable careers?

The same themes kept resurfacing. Ownership. Leverage. Streamlining. Sustaining.

Conversations with colleagues revealed that these issues weren't limited to songwriters. They were even more pronounced in touring, ticketing, agencies, streaming, merchandise, and now super-fan communities.

There's plenty of discussion around the Declaration of Independence, originally influenced by John Locke's phrase Life, Liberty, and the Pursuit of Property, later changed by Jefferson to the Pursuit of Happiness. I reference this not for political debate, but to underscore the enduring importance of ownership, worth, and self-sustainability.

Now, with the rise of AI, Web3, and blockchain, we stand at the edge of another seismic shift.

Historically, royalties have been distributed using market-share models. Performing rights organizations collect blanket licenses from venues without knowing exactly which songs were played, then distribute funds based on estimates. Radio has never paid strictly per play, and streaming still largely does not.

Payments are based on market share. That's why major labels and PROs receive money even when specific songs generate little or nothing.

But that system is changing.

Whether we like it or not, the natural evolution is toward direct, per-play royalty payments. If your song streams in India, the revenue could hit your account within 24 hours, minus minimal fees, bypassing legacy administration banking inefficiencies.

Why does this matter? Because the market-share model the industry, and investors, built their empires on may slowly disappear.

AI systems will track music usage everywhere and route payments directly to creators via blockchain-based systems with far fewer intermediaries. That shift could radically alter catalog values and raises the possibility that those who sold early, Dylans and Springsteens included, may have been the smartest players in the room after all.

Either way, massive change is coming.

My goal is simple. Bring clarity, leverage, and freedom back to the inventors of music.

Chapter Summary

- Reframes songwriters and artists as creators of a highly undervalued yet resilient asset class
- Explains why Wall Street and institutional investors aggressively acquired song catalogs
- Breaks down how investors view royalties as uncorrelated, long-term assets
- Encourages creators to adopt investor-level thinking without surrendering ownership
- Draws on personal experience to challenge the default narrative of selling catalogs
- Explores alternatives such as leveraging catalogs through loans and collective investment structures
- Examines how AI, Web3, and blockchain may reshape royalty infrastructure

- Introduces the possibility of real-time, per-play royalty distribution
- Questions the sustainability of legacy market-share payout models
- Calls on creators to reclaim ownership, create value, streamline systems, and build long-term financial freedom

Chapter 6

A Little Housekeeping

If you want to see an artist or songwriter immediately clam up and watch their palms get sweaty, just start talking about songwriting splits.

This book isn't a how-to guide or a music marketing manual. It's about self-worth, leverage, and understanding the true value of what you create. Still, there are a few conversations in our industry that lack basic clarity, and this is one of them. Consider this chapter a necessary bit of housekeeping.

Writing Splits and the Illusion of Scarcity

Songwriting splits have historically been a breeding ground for distrust, and for good reason. In darker chapters of industry history, songwriting credit was sometimes taken through coercion, ignorance, or empty promises. A "new car" that turned out to be a rental.

Bob Marley learned this early. When he signed with Cayman Music, the fine print granted the label songwriting credit and publishing. Marley responded creatively, crediting friends and family members as writers to protect his work. One of those credits went to Vincent Ford, a friend who ran a soup kitchen in Kingston, Jamaica. *No Woman, No Cry* wasn't just a song. It was a quiet act of resistance and generosity.

Chuck Berry faced similar exploitation. When he released *Maybellene* in 1955, songwriting credit was split with DJ Alan Freed, who received publishing simply for playing the song, and Leonard Chess, who took 25 percent of the writer's share despite Berry being the sole author. Those credits were eventually reversed, but the damage had already been done. Even the most successful artists aren't immune.

During the creation of *Say, Say, Say*, Paul McCartney famously explained music publishing to Michael Jackson, who later went on to buy the Beatles' catalog. Whether this story is tragic irony or business genius depends on perspective, but the real lesson is this. Lack of knowledge is not limited to struggling artists. Even global superstars can misunderstand their own value.

As the Spotify era emerged, major labels cemented the value of master income, which began to dwarf songwriter income. Labels received enormous upfront fees and equity stakes in Spotify. The downstream effect of lower streaming royalties created a divide-and-conquer culture that pits writers against one another, resulting in bloated co-writes and endless fights over percentages. If the pie were split fairly, much of that conflict would disappear.

Some of the greatest bands understood this instinctively.

Lennon and McCartney split everything 50/50. U2, Rush, and The Tragically Hip followed similar philosophies. I'm not saying this works in every scenario, but if you've ever seen a band fall apart, it's usually over this issue.

I prefer the Nashville approach. "Add a word, get a third." You contribute more in some rooms, less in others, but everyone leaves whole. The only real writing disputes I've experienced were outside of country music, primarily in pop sessions, particularly LA-style rooms. It's important to note that in oder to change a song or add another co-writer to it after the fact requires permission from all original songwriters first.

I once heard a story about the late Canadian producer Bruce Fairbairn, who refused to take songwriting credit even when he contributed meaningfully to the composition. His reasoning was simple. Artists create differently when they know the producer isn't trying to take a piece of their song. The result was a lifetime of producer royalties from landmark albums by Bon Jovi, Aerosmith, AC/DC, and Van Halen. Integrity scaled.

Who Actually Runs the Company?

One final clarification.

The artist does not work for the manager.

The artist is the CEO.

Managers propose ideas, use their connections, and handle day-to-day execution. Agents curate and negotiate live performance contracts. Lawyers protect interests. Producers create environments.

But the artist absorbs information from every direction and makes the final decision. That responsibility cannot be outsourced.

The Swift Blueprint

If you want a modern, undeniable example of ownership done right, look no further than Taylor Swift.

When negotiating her deal with Universal Music Group, Swift didn't just advocate for herself. She required the label to pay all outstanding royalties owed to every artist on the roster before she would sign. That wasn't public relations. That was leverage backed by clarity.

Earlier, when Big Machine Label Group used her masters as leverage, offering to return ownership only if she re-signed, Swift refused. The label responded by selling her masters to Scooter Braun without giving her the option to buy them, as was their contractual right.

The message was clear. We own your legacy.

Swift answered with action.

She re-recorded her catalog, legally, creatively, and strategically, under *Taylor's Version*. Fans followed. Sync buyers followed. The originals lost relevance. She didn't protest the system. She bypassed it. Eventually, she even bought back the original masters.

Taylor Swift didn't win because she was angry. She won because she was informed, prepared, and willing to walk away.

That's the point of this chapter: when you understand ownership, you either have a seat at the table, or you're on the menu.

Upstreaming and the Disguised Promotion

Let's talk about a term quietly gaining traction. Upstreaming.

Upstreaming functions similarly to a performance clause. If an artist performs well under an independent deal with major-label distribution or a joint-venture agreement, the major-label partner can "upstream" that artist into a direct deal.

It sounds like a promotion.

In reality, this is often the moment artists lose leverage, ownership of their masters, and in some cases publishing, copyright, or the dreaded 360 deal. These deals emerged after the damage Napster did to the legacy recording industry. The logic went something like this. We're losing money on recordings, so now we need a piece of everything the artist makes.

History shows there are alternatives if you understand leverage.

David Geffen, for example, did not sign an option allowing MCA to buy his company at the end of their term. He forced a full acquisition at term, at a premium, for $550 million. He immediately went on to start another label, DGC, where he signed Nirvana, Weezer, Sonic Youth, and Beck.

In the same way, an artist who builds real value does not have to accept an upstreaming clause. Success creates options. Shopping the deal. Renegotiating terms. Declining renewal. Triggering a bidding war. Or releasing independently.

Going independent means doing most of the work. It also means needing only a fraction of the success of a major-label artist to make the same money, if you own and leverage everything properly.

Leverage only exists if you know you have it.

Chapter Summary

- This chapter dismantles the confusion around songwriting splits, and the illusion of scarcity that fuels conflict in the music industry.

- Through real examples, it shows how lack of ownership knowledge costs creators leverage—even at the highest levels.

- True power belongs to the artist as CEO, not the surrounding infrastructure.

- When you understand ownership, leverage stops being theoretical and starts becoming optional.

Chapter 7

The Origin of Royalty Administration

Before Spotify was paying fractions of a penny per stream, before record labels perfected the 360 deal, before "exposure" became the most abused word in the creative economy, there was an earlier system doing the exact same thing, just with paper, pianos, and living rooms.

It was called Tin Pan Alley.

From the late 1800s into the early 1900s, Tin Pan Alley was America's songwriting factory.

A few blocks in New York City where composers sat in small offices, banging out songs the way factory workers punched a clock. The goal wasn't self-expression. It wasn't truth. It wasn't even artistry as we think about it now. The job was simple. Write something catchy enough to sell sheet music.

These writers weren't entrepreneurs. They weren't owners. They were employees, hired hands paid to manufacture melodies that middle-class families could play on upright pianos after dinner.

Tin Pan Alley wasn't serving artists or performers. It wasn't even serving listeners. It was serving a very specific customer: the white, literate, middle class.

Owning a piano was a status symbol. Learning to play, especially for daughters, was a sign of refinement. Families gathered around the instrument, played through the hits, sang the lyrics, and imagined themselves as the star of the show. They weren't buying music. They were buying the fantasy of being the artist.

Meanwhile, the real artists, blues musicians, folk storytellers, jazz innovators, immigrants bringing new rhythms and melodies into American culture, were largely invisible. Not because they didn't exist, but because Tin Pan Alley didn't know how to package them.

If your music couldn't be printed, sanitized, and sold to a piano-bench crowd, it didn't enter the machine. That was the first lesson of the modern music business. Value isn't determined by creativity. It's determined by who the system is built to serve.

When Music Was Declared Labor

In 1914, something changed.

ASCAP, the American Society of Composers, Authors and Publishers, was formed to do something radical for its time: recognize that music has ongoing value. Not just at the moment of sale, but every time it's performed publicly.

The idea was simple.

If a theater, restaurant, or broadcaster made money using your music, you deserved to be paid again. Not once. Not as a courtesy. But as a right.

ASCAP was deeply flawed. It was elitist. Exclusive. Controlled by the same Tin Pan Alley gatekeepers who had already decided which voices mattered. If you didn't fit the mold, you weren't getting in.

ASCAP was still defending a principle that mattered: music is labor, and labor deserves compensation every time it's exploited. That principle mattered because once you lose it, you don't get it back easily.

When Radio Took Control

By the 1930s, radio had become the most powerful distribution system music had ever seen. Free music. Everywhere. All the time. Broadcasters like CBS and NBC were making enormous profits selling advertising against songs they didn't create.

ASCAP said: you're using our members' work all day long. Pay for it.

In 1940, ASCAP attempted to raise licensing fees to better reflect the value radio was extracting.

That's when the broadcasters showed their hand. Instead of negotiating, instead of sharing more of the upside, they did what corporations always do when creators ask for fair compensation. They built a workaround. In 1939, the

National Association of Broadcasters created BMI, Broadcast Music, Inc.

The official story says BMI was formed to give opportunities to underrepresented music: blues, gospel, country, jazz, Latin. And yes, some of that happened. But let's not confuse outcomes with intentions. BMI wasn't created to empower creators. It was created to lower costs.

The buyers of music, the broadcasters, built their own rights organization so they could control both the pipeline and the price.

The Blackout That Changed Everything

In January 1941, ASCAP's catalog was pulled from radio entirely. For ten months, major stations refused to play ASCAP music. Listeners heard only BMI songs.

Some of that music was new. Some of it was exciting. But the real victory had nothing to do with creativity. The broadcasters won because they proved something devastatingly effective. If you control distribution, you control value.

Performance royalties were slashed. Exposure replaced compensation. And the narrative shifted. This wasn't framed as a loss for creators. It was sold as progress. As inclusion. As a win for music. It wasn't. It was a corporate heist dressed up as diversity.

The Blueprint We Never Escaped

It's tempting to romanticize this era, to see BMI as a rebellion against ASCAP's old gatekeepers. BMI wasn't a revolution for creators. It was a revolution for buyers who didn't want to keep paying them.

ASCAP, for all its flaws, was still defending the idea that music is work. But BMI's purpose was simpler: to introduce competition, reduce costs, and further erode songwriter earnings.

Once broadcasters owned the rights infrastructure, creators never fully regained leverage. And if this story feels familiar, it should. Because this is the same model we're living under today. Streaming didn't invent exploitation. It refined it.

Spotify didn't stumble into paying pennies. It inherited a blueprint drawn decades earlier, the moment the people who were supposed to pay creators figured out how to set the price themselves. That's when music stopped being treated as labor and started being treated as content.

Sold, Slowly

This is what giving away worth actually looks like.

Not all at once.

Not with a single bad deal.

But inch by inch.

License by license.

Song by song.

Until one day you look around and realize your work is everywhere, in homes, cars, phones, restaurants, hospitals, and cities, and you're still struggling to survive.

That's not an accident.

It's not incompetence.

And it's not the market.

It's design.

And unless we understand where that design came from, we'll keep repeating it, smiling politely, grateful for exposure, while being sold for a song.

The Modern Black Box

More recently, Jeff Price, founder of TuneCore, Audiam, and Word Collection, has become one of the most outspoken critics of the modern royalty collection system.

He has called the Mechanical Licensing Collective a "black hole for song data," citing how song registrations are routinely ignored or lost.

"We submitted thousands of works," he writes, "and got zero confirmation or visibility. It's like sending music into the void."

Despite the Music Modernization Act's promise to fix the system, Price argues it's business as usual, just centralized.

"Roughly 25 percent of mechanicals are still withheld," he

notes. "That's nearly $600 million sitting unpaid. Nothing has changed."

His most serious claim is that the MLC's backend partner, the Harry Fox Agency, redirected royalties from his company to its own subsidiary.

"They deleted our banking details and sent the checks elsewhere," he says.

His takeaway is blunt.

"The system wasn't designed for songwriters. It was designed to protect incumbents."

Why We Still Don't Have Transparent Pay-For-Play

Listen to legendary Hall of Fame songwriter Roger Cook share on my podcast how, for years, he received the same check annually from his PRO.

The same amount. Every year.

What are the odds that every song he wrote earned exactly the same amount of money annually?

When a bar or restaurant pays an annual performance license for the music they use and profit from, and the PROs collect that money, who gets paid?

Who is tracking every song played in a restaurant or live music bar?

The answer is nobody.

So where does the money go?

It gets pooled. Estimated. Distributed by market share.

It was probably a Beatles song. Or the Rolling Stones. Or Elton John. So the money gets split and sent accordingly.

The same logic applies to radio and streaming.

The legacy system is a market-share, non-transparent system.

Now add Wall Street investors and pension funds who have spent hundreds of millions, even billions, purchasing catalogs.

What happens when true usage data emerges through AI tracking, intermediaries are removed by blockchain and Web3, and payments become direct?

The entire earnings model will be exposed.

And with it, the realization that the so-called undervalued song world may no longer be getting paid based on what those catalogs were actually worth.

Chapter Summary

•This chapter traces how music shifted from craft to commodity, beginning with Tin Pan Alley and accelerating through radio, PROs, and corporate control.

•What started as recognizing music as labor slowly became a system where buyers set the price and creators lost leverage.

•From BMI to streaming, the same blueprint repeats: distribution controls value, and exposure replaces pay.

•Until creators understand this design, music will keep being everywhere—and still sold for a song.

Chapter 8

The Leverage Gap

For decades, artists were told the same story: *Just focus on the art. Someone else will handle the business. This is how it's always worked.* What no one explained is that while you were focused on creating, everyone else was focused on leverage.

Leverage isn't a dirty word. It isn't manipulation. It isn't greed. Leverage simply answers one question: **Who benefits most from your work?** Right now, in most creative careers, the answer isn't the artist.

It's the platform.

The distributor.

The publisher.

The label.

The tech company.

The advertiser.

Your music. Your identity. Your audience. Your data. All generating value, while you're paid last, least, or not at all.

This didn't happen by accident.

Leverage lives in two places: **ownership and access**. Who owns the relationship with your audience? Who owns the data created by their behavior? Who controls the systems that monetize attention? Who benefits from the long tail of your work?

For most artists, the uncomfortable truth is this: they create the value, but they don't control the context in which that value is monetized.

Historically, artists were trained to trade leverage for opportunity. Sign this to get exposure. Give this up to get access. Hand this over to go to the next level.

For a long time, those trades were framed as necessary. And in earlier eras, they often were. Distribution was scarce. Infrastructure was expensive. Gatekeepers controlled access to the market.

But the real cost of those trades was never made explicit. Every time leverage was exchanged for opportunity, the artist's future became more fragile. Not immediately. Quietly. Over time.

The Billboard Illusion

Most artists believe platforms are the destination. Streaming. Social media. Discovery algorithms. They're not. They are billboards. Billboards don't build businesses. They direct traffic.

The tragedy is that artists were never told they could own the destination. So instead of guiding people toward something they control, they send fans deeper into systems designed to extract value, not return it.

Every click teaches the platform more about your audience than you'll ever be allowed to know. That information becomes leverage, just not yours.

Visibility without ownership creates dependence. Reach without direction creates exhaustion. When artists confuse exposure with leverage, they become incredibly efficient at enriching systems that were never designed to serve them.

Why "Superfans" Miss the Point

The industry loves the word *superfans* now. Kiss and their Kiss Army wrote the book on superfans back in the 1970s.

But the real shift isn't about fans becoming more loyal. It's about artists becoming more self-directed.

Leverage doesn't come from asking fans to do more. It comes from structuring your world so your work finally works for you.

When leverage is aligned:

- fans don't feel sold to

- value feels natural
- money becomes an exchange, not a chase

This isn't about hype. It's about alignment.

And there may be no clearer example of this than the career of Loreena McKennitt.

The Loreena McKennitt Lesson

Loreena McKennitt grew up in Manitoba, Canada, far from the commercial centers of the music industry. From the beginning, she was drawn to the harp and traditional Celtic, folk, and world music, a lane that, at the time, had almost no obvious commercial pathway.

When she moved to Toronto in the early 1980s, she performed wherever she could, subway stations, folk clubs, small halls, churches, and community events.

She financed her early recordings herself, pressing cassettes and vinyl in small runs and selling records directly after shows, literally hand to hand. No label. No industry machinery. Just songs, audience connection, and relentless consistency.

In 1985, she made a defining decision: she founded her own label, Quinlan Road. No one else understood her music well enough, or valued it properly, to steward it.

As her audience grew internationally, something unusual happened. Albums rooted in ancient texts, poetry, and non-mainstream arrangements began selling in astonishing numbers, particularly in Europe.

By industry logic, this was the moment to “level up,” to sign a major deal, hire a powerful manager, or hand control to people with leverage.

Loreena did the opposite.

Instead of entering the traditional manager, agent, label hierarchy, she built her own internal team handling management, touring logistics, booking, operations, and long-term strategy.

This wasn’t a branding statement. It was a control statement. Ownership of her recordings. Alignment with her values. A team that served the work, not the industry’s expectations.

By every conventional metric, Loreena McKennitt was “unmarketable.” No radio singles. No pop structure. No industry machine. No mainstream press push.

And yet, she went on to sell tens of millions of albums worldwide, becoming one of the best-selling independent artists of all time.

The key wasn’t scale. It was trust.

Her audience trusted the authenticity of the work, the consistency of her output, and the direct relationship she maintained with listeners. And because she owned her masters, controlled her touring, and managed her business internally, success didn’t dilute her leverage. It compounded it.

Loreena McKennitt didn't wage war on the music industry. She simply opted out of its default power structures.

No manifesto. No crusade. Just a long, disciplined career built on ownership, patience, internal infrastructure, and respect for the music itself.

Her story proves something most artists are never told: **you don't need permission to build your own system. You need clarity about what you're protecting.**

That is leverage.

The Dolly Quotient

Dolly Parton is often described as a cultural icon, a songwriter, or a national treasure. What's less discussed is that she may be the most disciplined ownership strategist modern music has ever produced.

Not because she chased leverage or talked about business openly, but because she quietly built a career where she never needed permission, from labels, managers, or the market, to decide what her work was worth.

The foundation of that strategy was simple: she wrote her own songs. Almost all of them. Alone.

In an industry built on splits, committees, and dilution, Dolly created complete works, songs with no co-writers, no fractured rights, and no downstream friction. Each song wasn't just a creative expression. It was a fully intact asset.

Because she wrote alone, she owned the publishing. And because she owned the publishing, she owned time. Publishing didn't just pay Dolly. It gave her patience.

She didn't need to chase moments, rush decisions, or trade long-term value for short-term opportunity. Her songs worked for her whether she was on stage or not, whether she was current or not, whether the industry shifted or not.

When Elvis Presley wanted to record *I Will Always Love You*, the deal came with a request for a cut of the publishing. Dolly said no. Not out of ego or stubbornness, but out of clarity.

She understood that a great song doesn't need a great moment. It needs longevity. Years later, that same song became one of the most successful recordings in history, under terms she fully controlled.

What looked like restraint was actually leverage maturing.

That patience extended beyond music. When she built Dollywood, she wasn't licensing her name. She was investing in infrastructure. Something tangible. Something that didn't depend on trends, radio, or relevance cycles.

Dolly never framed herself as a business genius. She didn't evangelize strategy or posture as a mogul. She simply behaved like someone who respected her work enough to protect it.

That restraint, quiet, consistent, and long-term, is what allowed her to avoid the traps that swallowed so many of her peers. In today's climate, creators are told that selling their catalog is inevitable, even wise. Dolly's career is living proof that this isn't true.

She never needed the payday because she never sold the engine. Her catalog did exactly what it was supposed to do: provide freedom, stability, and choice, without surrendering control.

Dolly Parton didn't just make music that lasted. She made decisions that aged well. And in an industry obsessed with speed, that may be the most radical form of self-worth there is.

Leverage Before Efficiency

This is where many creators get it wrong.

They try to streamline before they control anything.

But if you streamline a system you don't own, all you're doing is becoming more efficient for someone else.

Without leverage:

- speed increases dependency
- growth increases exhaustion
- success increases fragility

Leverage must come first.

Only after you answer *who this is really serving* does efficiency actually help you.

. . .

Ownership of Context

The future of creative careers isn't about more followers. It's about ownership of context.

Owning where your work lives.

How it's experienced.

How value flows.

How relationships deepen.

Leverage is the difference between being included and being in control.

Not control over people. Control over your path.

Why This Changes Everything

When you retain leverage, negotiations change. Partnerships change. Sustainability becomes possible.

You stop chasing permission.

You stop trading your future for access.

You stop confusing opportunity with obligation.

And when larger systems come calling, labels, platforms, promoters, you meet them from alignment, not desperation.

That is the difference between being discovered and being prepared.

Chapter Summary

- Leverage determines who benefits most from your work
- Leverage lives in ownership and access
- Platforms are billboards, not destinations
- Artists were trained to trade leverage for opportunity
- Scale without control is fragile
- Leverage must come before streamlining

Chapter 9

Streamlining: Taking Back Your Time

Every artist I know wants the same thing: more time to create, more space to think, more energy to feel alive in their work again.

And yet, the more "successful" they become, the less time they have.

In **The Rest Ethic**, **Dr. Sean Orr** challenges the modern obsession with productivity and hustle, arguing that rest is not the opposite of work, but a prerequisite for meaningful contribution. As he writes:

"Rest is not a reward for finishing your work. It is the condition that makes good work possible."

That single idea reframed everything for me.

Most creative burnout isn't caused by lack of discipline or ambition. It's caused by systems that treat humans like machines, extracting output without protecting recovery.

When rest is removed from the equation, creativity doesn't scale, it collapses.

What Dr. Orr makes clear is that exhaustion is not a personal failure. It's a structural consequence of environments that value constant motion over sustainable creation. Rest isn't laziness. It's resistance. It's where clarity returns, intuition sharpens, and meaning reconnects to the work.

Seen through that lens, streamlining isn't just about efficiency. It's about **restoring the conditions that allow creativity to exist at all.**

The Myth of Productivity

Artists aren't exhausted because they're lazy. They're exhausted because they're carrying too many roles.

Creator.

Marketer.

Administrator.

Manager.

Strategist.

Customer support.

None of which were the reason they started.

Streamlining isn't about doing more. It's about removing resistance.

. . .

Why Burnout Is Structural, Not Personal

Burnout is often framed as a mindset issue. It's not. It's a systems issue.

When your life requires constant decision-making, context-switching, and emotional labor, your creativity doesn't disappear. It retreats.

Not because it's gone. Because it's protecting itself.

Time Is the Real Currency

Money can be earned again. Momentum can return. But time only moves in one direction.

Every unnecessary task steals attention, fragments energy, and dulls intuition.

Streamlining is about protecting the conditions creativity needs to survive.

The Difference Between Busy and Effective

Busy artists chase validation. Effective artists build environments.

The goal isn't to be everywhere. It's to create a center of gravity, a place where your work, your voice, and your audience converge naturally.

Streamlining creates fewer decisions, clearer priorities, longer creative stretches, and sustainable momentum.

Not speed. Flow.

Why Streamlining Feels Uncomfortable

Because chaos feels familiar.

Many creatives were trained in disorder:

last-minute pressure

reactive decisions

survival-mode urgency

Streamlining can feel like loss at first.

But what you're really losing is noise, distraction, obligation, fragmentation.

And what you gain is presence.

Streamlining Is Permission

Permission to stop explaining yourself.

Permission to stop chasing everything.

Permission to stop proving your worth.

Permission to stop doing work that drains you.

It's not about control. It's about alignment.

. . .

Chapter Summary

- Burnout is structural, not personal
- Time is the most valuable creative asset
- Streamlining removes friction, not creativity
- Busy is not the same as effective
- Simplification restores momentum
- Creativity thrives in protected space

Chapter 10

Neurodiversity and Creativity

One day, my ex-wife watched me slowly lose my mind while trying to assemble IKEA furniture, instructions spread everywhere, frustration rising by the minute. What started as a simple moment of embarrassment turned into a conversation about my lifelong, so-called learning disability.

That conversation led to a realization that would quietly change the course of my life.

Mental health has become a popular topic in the arts, and I believe the reason is far simpler than most explanations suggest.

According to statistics, over half of American households have at least one person who can sing or play an instrument. In other words, musical ability itself is not rare. So the question becomes: why Mozart? Why Prince? Why Jimi Hendrix?

Beyond work ethic, what truly sets them apart?

I'm willing to go out on a limb and suggest that what we often label as "mental health struggles" in creatives, especially the most gifted ones, may actually be the source of their extraordinary perception and originality.

Could this also be the root of the low self-worth so many creatives carry? And does neurodiversity play a larger role in how we come to value ourselves than we've been willing to admit?

To explore this further, I turn to the work of Dr. Gabor Maté, a physician widely respected for his research on trauma, ADHD, and emotional development.

Maté challenges the conventional understanding of ADHD, arguing that it is not a disease or a genetic defect, but a neurodevelopment response to early stress. He explains that ADHD emerges as a coping mechanism, a way the developing brain adapts when a child experiences emotional distress or a lack of attuned caregiving.

In this view, the same neurological traits that make sustained focus difficult can also become powerful creative tools when properly understood and supported.

Maté has pointed out that many highly creative individuals think non-linearly. Their minds make connections others overlook. These traits, intuition, rapid association, sensitivity, and deep emotional awareness, are often present in artists, inventors, and entrepreneurs.

What society labels as dysfunction may actually be unrecognized capacity.

However, when these traits are misunderstood or punished early in life, they frequently manifest as anxiety, emotional disregulation, and low self-esteem. Many people with ADHD grow up feeling different, broken, or behind. Over time, this can develop into chronic self-doubt, rejection sensitivity, and shame.

Maté also connects ADHD to patterns of addiction and self-medication. When the nervous system struggles to regulate dopamine and emotional stress, individuals often seek relief through substances, food, technology, or constant stimulation. These behaviors are not moral failures. They are attempts to self-soothe an overwhelmed system.

Depression and hopelessness can follow, especially after years of unmet expectations, academically, professionally, or relationally.

Add to this a difficulty staying present, a restless mind, and strained relationships, and it becomes clear why so many creatives wrestle with mental health challenges while simultaneously producing extraordinary work.

Importantly, Maté does not frame ADHD as something to be "fixed," but something to be understood and healed.

Healing, in his view, involves addressing the nervous system, cultivating self-awareness, and replacing self-criticism with self-compassion. Practices such as mindfulness, somatic therapy, movement, creative expression, and supportive relationships all play a role.

Medication, he suggests, can be useful for some, but it should not be the only solution. Without emotional healing and lifestyle alignment, symptom management alone misses the deeper issue.

When viewed through this lens, ADHD, and neurodiversity more broadly, is not a disorder of deficiency. It is a different way of processing the world. A way that, when supported rather than suppressed, often produces the very creativity, empathy, and innovation society depends on.

Perhaps the real tragedy is not that so many creatives struggle with self-worth, but that they were never taught that the very traits they were trying to overcome might be the source of their greatest value.

Chapter Summary

- Creativity is common, but exceptional creative output often comes from minds that think differently, not linearly

- Neurodiversity, particularly ADHD traits, may be an adaptive response to early stress rather than a defect or disease

- Many creatives internalize low self-worth because their neurological differences are misunderstood or punished early in life

- The same brain traits linked to distraction and restlessness can also drive intuition, pattern recognition, and innovation

• Anxiety, emotional dysregulation, addiction, and depression in creatives are often coping responses, not character flaws

• ADHD-related challenges frequently stem from nervous system dysregulation and unresolved emotional stress

• Healing involves self-awareness, trauma-informed care, mindfulness, movement, and supportive relationships, not just symptom control

• Medication can be helpful for some, but it should not replace emotional healing and lifestyle alignment

• Reframing ADHD as a difference rather than a disorder restores self-compassion and personal value

• When creatives understand and honor how their minds work, perceived weaknesses can become their greatest strengths

Chapter 11

How Artists and Fans Can Game The System

There was a time when discovering and supporting an artist followed a simple, physical path. You heard a song on the radio, saw a performance on television, or noticed an ad in print. If the music stayed with you, you went to your local record store and sifted through the bins.

The experience was organic. The exchange was simple. And while intermediaries existed, the relationship between artist and fan still felt human.

Today, discovery is everywhere.

The value of music has plummeted. What once cost $15 for an album now buys unlimited access to nearly all recorded music for $15 a month. Songs surface on playlists, feeds, and short-form videos. Access has exploded, but connection has quietly eroded.

Fans hear more music than ever, yet know less about the artists behind it. Artists, in turn, are surrounded by audiences they cannot see, understand, or reach without permission.

So what does meaningful support look like now?

The future of the artist and fan relationship is not built on being overleveraged. It is built on direct connection.

The artist of today must deliver an entertainment and connection experience unlike anything in history.

The Private Portal

The most powerful way fans can experience and support the artists they care about is by bypassing intermediaries entirely and going straight to the source.

What most people still call a website, I call an artist's **private portal**.

A private portal is not a marketing page. It is a world.

It is a place owned and controlled by the artist, where music lives alongside story, purpose, and context. A space where fans are not treated as data points or impressions, but as participants in a shared ecosystem.

It is a home where artists can live from their unique blueprint and serve others through the revealing experience of song.

When built intentionally, a private portal offers a level of access, value, and depth that no platform can replicate.

Here is the best part: you do not need another tech company to build this for you.

With your own knowledge, and AI streamlining solutions most artists can build and maintain the infrastructure they need quite easily.

When the common language shifts from platform-first to artist-direct, everything changes.

Ticket sales.

Merchandise.

Special releases.

Limited editions.

Experiences.

These no longer need to pass through layers of extraction before reaching the people who actually care.

The artist sets the tone.

The artist defines the relationship.

And the fan receives something far richer in return.

We are only a few years away from being able to speak our entire software solution into a phone and have it built for us. The technology is not the barrier. Ownership is.

If I see one more software solution for creatives that takes a percentage of earnings, I might lose my mind.

This isn't rocket science.

Own.

Leverage.

Streamline.

Sustain.

Will you build every possible solution inside your portal? No.

But you can own and control the majority of the infrastructure required to sustain a career.

Make it painfully easy for the world to find your portal, and the right fans will find you.

Why Platforms Resist This

This shift exposes an uncomfortable truth about the current system.

Social media platforms actively discourage direct relationships.

Post a link to your website and reach mysteriously drops. Engagement softens. Visibility shrinks.

The message is subtle but consistent: stay here. Don't remind people that you exist beyond the feed.

That isn't a technical flaw. It is the business model.

Platforms want to be the destination. Artists were never meant to be.

Fans were trained, slowly and quietly, to believe that discovery means remaining inside someone else's ecosystem. Scroll. Tap. Save. Repeat.

The moment an artist asks a fan to step outside that system, friction appears.

This is why the entire philosophy of discovery needs to change.

If you hear a song you love, on TikTok, in a playlist, through a recommendation, the most powerful move is not clicking follow.

If there is no link in the bio, it is opening a browser and searching for the artist's private portal. Going directly to their world.

That single action bypasses monopolies, market-share gatekeepers, and algorithmic toll booths designed to stand between creator and audience.

And what should be waiting there is not a generic landing page.

It should feel like entering another dimension. An immersive environment built around the values, curiosity, and creative gravity of a specific human being, or group of human beings.

A place where music is not compressed into content, but expanded into meaning. Where value is felt, not extracted.

This is the experience fans are actually waiting for, whether they realize it yet or not.

. . .

Rendering Platforms Optional

This future does not build itself.

If artists want fans to come directly to them, there is work to be done.

A private portal must be easy to find. Easy to navigate. And unmistakably personal.

Discovery does not disappear. It relocates. From platforms back to people.

The only way creators and fans truly move around monopolies and market-share gatekeepers is by refusing to route their relationship through them in the first place.

Not by fighting platforms.

Not by negotiating slightly better terms.

But by rendering them optional.

This isn't rebellion. It's architecture.

Fans are ready. They are curious. They are hungry for depth in a world of compression.

The artist and fan relationship of the future is direct, intentional, and built on mutual respect.

Artists just need to meet fans halfway, with ownership, clarity, and a world worth stepping into.

. . .

Chapter Summary

- The traditional artist and fan relationship was once limited by physical distribution but remained human and intentional
- Platforms normalized limitless access while eroding perceived value and artist connection
- The future is built on direct relationships, not platform leverage
- An artist's private portal becomes the new center of gravity
- Platforms discourage outbound connection by design, not accident
- Discovery must shift from feeds back to people
- Ownership of infrastructure enables sustainable creative careers
- The path forward is architecture, not rebellion
- The future artist and fan relationship is immersive, intentional, and rooted in mutual respect

Chapter 12

The New Song Is You

For most of the history of the music business, the *song* was easy to define.

It was the composition.

The lyric.

The melody.

The master recording.

It lived on paper, on tape, on vinyl. You could point to it. Own it. Sell it.

That clarity is gone.

In the digital age, the song is no longer just the work you create.

The song is **you**.

Your behavior.

Your clicks.

Your likes.

Your location history.

Your private messages.

Your creative process.

All of it reduced to a constant stream of data points.

If you're a fan, your listening habits, comments, and even how long you hover over a track are data.

The system doesn't just distribute music anymore.

It **extracts information**.

And that changes everything.

From Undervalued Songs to Undervalued Humans

If the old *Sold 4 a Song* was about music being undervalued, the new *Sold 4 a Song* is about people being undervalued.

Your ideas.

Your identity.

Your intellectual fingerprints.

All mined, modeled, and monetized, often without your knowledge, let alone your consent.

Technologist and VR pioneer Jaron Lanier describes this reality bluntly. He calls us *data serfs*, individuals whose information is harvested, traded, and weaponized by systems we don't control.

What's taken from us is sold back in familiar forms:

Advertising.

Algorithmic feeds.

Behavioral nudges designed to keep us scrolling, clicking, reacting.

The extraction isn't just economic.

It's psychological.

And for creatives, the danger runs even deeper.

The BUMMER Machine

Lanier refers to today's digital system as the **BUMMER machine**:

Behaviors of Users Modified and Made into an Empire for Rent.

It works like this.

First, it captures your attention.

Then it amplifies whatever keeps you engaged the longest: outrage, fear, identity.

Finally, it monetizes that engagement by selling influence to the highest bidder.

But the most dangerous part isn't that it turns you into a product.

It's that it **rewires you**.

It shapes what you believe is important.

It nudges creativity toward what performs, not what's true.

It rewards reaction over reflection.

Communication becomes clickbait.

Empathy becomes emojis.

Disagreement becomes war.

For songwriters and artists, this is especially corrosive, because the system doesn't just manipulate your audience.

It manipulates **you**.

Quietly, it pulls your creative compass away from meaning and toward whatever produces the fastest hit of digital approval.

The Stakes Have Changed

In earlier eras, exploitation in creative industries was largely about compensation.

Royalty rates.

Ownership splits.

Contract terms.

Those battles still matter, but the terrain has shifted.

In the age of AI and big tech, we are no longer just protecting income streams. We are protecting the inputs that train the machines.

Our data.

Our process.

Our creative DNA.

Every prompt.

Every draft.

Every discarded idea.

The raw materials of human creativity are now the fuel for automated systems designed to scale without us.

That's a different level of risk.

Mediators of Individual Data

Lanier offers a concept that reframes the problem at a structural level: **M.I.D.s**, Mediators of Individual Data.

At its core, the idea is simple.

What if individuals, especially creators, had sovereignty over their digital selves?

Imagine a world where your ideas, work, and behavioral data weren't scattered across platforms, but stewarded through a structure that:

- recognizes authorship

- respects consent
- acknowledges ongoing value

Not as a product.

As a person.

Now imagine that principle operating collectively, not as isolated individuals negotiating against trillion-dollar companies, but as a coordinated body with shared leverage.

This isn't nostalgia for old unions.

It's an evolution of collective power for a new extraction economy.

Closing the Loop on *$0ld 4 a $ong*

The fight for fair value has always been about ownership.

Once, it was about publishing rights and master recordings.

Now, it's about owning the digital DNA of who we are and what we make.

The story comes full circle when we recognize this truth:

The same forces that once devalued songs are now devaluing human beings.

Creators and audiences alike.

We cannot afford to play the same game with higher stakes.

We need systems that respect the sanctity of work, attention, and identity.

Systems that see creators not as inventory, but as sovereign entities with dignity and rights.

That is the promise behind M.I.D.s.

That is the promise of a new form of collective leverage.

The Game Above the Game

For too long, creatives have been playing defense, trying to survive within rules written by someone else.

But here's the uncomfortable truth:

The rules are the problem.

The new mandate is to play the **game above the game**.

That means questioning the frameworks, terms of service, and abstractions designed by the very companies profiting from our compliance.

It means refusing to treat AI as a mystical force instead of what it actually is:

A network of people making profit-driven decisions.

Every algorithm is authored.

Every dataset is sourced.

Every outcome is chosen.

When technology hides behind abstraction, transparency becomes power.

Pull back the curtain and you don't find inevitability.

You find a boardroom.

The Compounding Threat, and the Counterforce

Behavior modifiers sit on one side.

Advertisers and influence buyers sit on the other.

Between them is a simple strategy:

Small nudges.

Massive scale.

Shift behavior by a few percentage points.

Tilt opinion slightly.

Alter buying habits just enough.

The effects compound.

Elections swing.

Markets move.

Cultures fracture.

That is the power they've perfected.

And it's the same power creators can reclaim, not through outrage, but through **structure**.

Community and coordination are leverage.

When creators pool their voices, their data, and their standards, extraction becomes harder. Manipulation becomes visible. Bad-faith actors lose access.

If we don't organize for this future, we leave the door open to an economy that treats every human as a resource to be mined.

Chapter Summary

- The definition of "the song" has expanded to include human data and behavior
- Digital platforms extract value from identity, attention, and creative process
- The BUMMER machine monetizes behavior, not just content
- AI systems are trained on human creativity, often without consent
- Ownership must evolve beyond songs to include digital selfhood
- Collective structures are necessary to counter extraction at scale

Chapter 13

Fear of Flying

Alanis Morissette, who in so many ways felt divinely placed in my life, once said something to me when I was struggling with the same old, debilitating lack of self worth. She looked at me and said:

"You need to take the words if, and, and but out of your vocabulary. You don't need them anymore."

At the time, I didn't fully understand how to tackle that task. I do now.

My life has slowly led me to a realization that feels both humbling and liberating:

You are the operant power.

Through the gift of free will, we create scarcity, fear, and worry in the same way we create happiness, meaning, and abundance. The mechanism is the same. Only the story changes.

Whether you call it God, Jesus, Buddha, Allah, Spirit, the Universe, Science, Quantum Mathematics, Star Wars, or Donkey, it doesn't matter. The language differs, but the insight is consistent. Across ancient wisdom and modern science, mystics and neuroscientists keep arriving at the same conclusion:

We are not cut off from possibility.

We are the source of it.

We all have access to far more than we allow ourselves to believe.

I've come to believe that our purpose isn't to discover meaning, it's to create it. Using our unique blueprint and the quiet, terrifying power of free will. And the cycle doesn't complete until that creation moves outward, until it serves others with the intention of awakening the same realization in them, without attachment to the outcome.

We are not victims.

We are limitless creatives.

And by that, I don't mean artists, painters, or musicians.

Creative is just another word for human.

A Story About Fear

We can waste a lifetime letting ego, fear, programming, victimhood, entitlement, and the lies we tell ourselves decide the size of our lives. Or we can remember who we actually are, not the résumé, not the trauma, not the approval rating, but the creative spirit we were uniquely shaped to be.

I want to close with a story, lighthearted, but true.

Years ago, I had the bucket list pleasure of producing a few big band orchestral albums at the legendary Capitol Studios in Los Angeles. A dream team. One of those rare moments where you know you're exactly where you're supposed to be.

One evening, while mixing my longtime friend, Canadian artist Matt Dusk, with the legendary Al Schmitt in Studio C, fellow Canadians David Foster and Michael Bublé were recording a new album in Studio A at the same time. They couldn't have been kinder.

They invited us over, shared quality time and dinner for a few days, and David even invited us to a party at Warner Music president Tom Whalley's house in Beverly Hills, where Matt Dusk and Michael performed a duet with David on piano.

At one point, we had some downtime in the studio, and I asked Michael a question I'd been genuinely curious about. I said:

"There are millions of singers in the world. But you can sell out the Staples Center in Los Angeles, twice in a single year. Why?"

He looked at me, slightly confused, and said, "What do you mean?"

I said, "What makes you different?"

He paused for a moment, then said something I didn't expect.

"I have a serious, unhealthy relationship with fear."

He went on, "If I realize I'm afraid of something, say flying, I'll drain my bank account, fly nonstop around the world, desert friends and family if I have to, no matter how long it takes, until the fear is gone."

I sat there for a second and said, "Let me get this straight."

You take humankind's oldest obstacle, fear, the biggest lie we tell ourselves, and you put conquering it at the top of your priority list until it no longer controls you?

"That's why you can sell out the Staples Center twice in one year."

What Fear Really Is

Fear of flying isn't about airplanes. It never is.

In fact, I went a decade without flying out of fear. The best part is that the day I decided to fly again was on a round the world trip that just happened to line up with 9/11. I was in Singapore and had to get on my flight to Australia the next morning.

My fear of flying was over for good.

I spoke to a wise medical intuitive back in the 1990s while on my no fly zone hiatus. She shared something that stayed with me:

"You're not afraid of flying. You're afraid to be successful, and flying represents new heights."

Fear is just the last illusion standing between who we are and who we're pretending to be.

Confidence is simply the byproduct of courage, courage to go into the darkness only to find the light that is always unconditionally waiting for us on the other side.

This book has been about value.

About leverage.

About streamlining.

About sustaining.

But underneath all of it was something quieter.

The fear of fully trusting ourselves.

The fear of worth.

The fear of flying.

And the moment we're willing to let that go, truly let it go, the question stops being:

What am I allowed to have?

It becomes:

What am I finally ready to create?

I don't remember who said it, but I believe this to my core:

"The two most important days of our lives are the day we are born, and the day we find out why."

THE END

With love and gratitude,

Terrance Lee Sawchuk

Epilogue

The Quiet Reckoning

If this book has done its job, it hasn't given you answers.

It's given you pause.

Pause to notice how easily value is handed away.

Pause to question the systems we inherit without consent.

Pause to recognize the quiet moments where worth was decided for you, by contracts, platforms, expectations, or fear.

Most creators never lose their worth in one dramatic moment.

They lose it gradually.

In small compromises.

In unchecked assumptions.

In deals that feel "good enough" at the time.

And yet, worth has never truly left you.

It was only buried beneath urgency, noise, and a culture that rewards initiative over fairness.

No system will ever protect your value better than you will.

No gatekeeper will ever care more about your work than you do.

And no amount of exposure can replace ownership, clarity, and intention.

This isn't a call to reject the world or burn down the industry.

It's a call to stand differently within it.

To ask better questions.

You don't need permission to value yourself.

Somewhere along the way, many of us were taught that survival requires surrender.

That passion should be its own reward.

That wanting more, more respect, more fairness, somehow makes you difficult or ungrateful.

It doesn't.

It makes you awake.

The future of creative work won't be decided by technology alone.

It will be decided by the individual choices creators make every day,

what they keep,

what they give away,

and what they finally refuse to sell.

If there's one thing worth carrying forward, it's this:

Your work has value because you do.

And reclaiming that truth doesn't start with a contract, a platform, or a strategy.

It starts with remembering who you are,

before you were ever asked to sell yourself for a song.

Acknowledgements

This book exists because of countless conversations, moments of grace, and people who crossed my path at exactly the right time.

To the artists, songwriters, musicians, producers, engineers, and creatives who trusted me with their stories, thank you. Your honesty, resilience, and courage shaped this work more than you know.

To the mentors who taught me through example, sometimes by what to do, sometimes by what not to do, I am grateful for every lesson.

To the friends who listened while I wrestled with doubt, clarity, and conviction, thank you for holding space when I needed it most.

And to those who challenged me, resisted these ideas, or forced me to sharpen my thinking, you helped make this book stronger.

To the readers willing to question inherited systems and reclaim their worth, this book is for you.

To Paul, you were my first fan, support system, and believer in my music.

To Neville, you taught me how to leave anger to God.

To Sean, I feel healthiest simply being in your presence.

To my late father and my 97 year young mother, thank you for creating an environment that allowed me to dream without judgment.

To Gunnar, the answer to many prayers, thank you for showing me what God's will feels like.

Finally, to the love of my life, my match in every sense of the word, Jennifer, thank you for being my sounding board, my incubator, and most of all, my safe place to land at the end of each day.

About the Author

Terrance Lee Sawchuk is a Billboard #1, multi-platinum songwriter, producer, artist, recording and mixing engineer who has spent more than thirty-five years inside the trenches of the music business. *$old 4 a $ong* comes from that long view, an examination of ownership, worth, and the unseen systems that turn creative labor into product while slowly teaching the people who make it to accept less than they're worth.

www.ingramcontent.com/pod-product-compliance
Ingram Content Group UK Ltd.
Pitfield, Milton Keynes, MK11 3LW, UK
UKHW040042200726
13854UKWH00001B/493